W9-APS-265

# Oviraptor/Oviraptor

By **Joanne Mattern**
**Illustrations by Jeffrey Mangiat**

**Reading Consultant:** Susan Nations, M.Ed.,
author/literacy coach/consultant in literacy development
**Science Consultant:** Darla Zelenitsky, Ph.D.,
Assistant Professor of Dinosaur Paleontology at the University of Calgary, Canada

**WEEKLY READER®**
PUBLISHING

Please visit our web site at www.garethstevens.com.
For a free color catalog describing our list of high-quality books,
call 1-800-542-2595 (USA) or 1-800-387-3178 (Canada).
Our fax: 1-877-542-2596

**Library of Congress Cataloging-in-Publication Data**

Mattern, Joanne, 1963–
　　[Oviraptor. Spanish & English]
　　Oviraptor / by Joanne Mattern ; illustrations by Jeffrey Mangiat / Oviraptor / por Joanne Mattern ;
ilustraciones de Jeffrey Mangiat.
　　　p. cm. — (Let's read about dinosaurs / Conozcamos a los dinosaurios)
　　Includes bibliographical references and index.
　　ISBN-10: 0-8368-9425-1　　ISBN-13: 978-0-8368-9425-7 (lib. bdg.)
　　ISBN-10: 0-8368-9429-4　　ISBN-13: 978-0-8368-9429-5 (softcover)
　　1. Oviraptor—Juvenile literature.　I. Title.
QE862.S3M33225518　　2009
567.912—dc22　　　　　　　　　　　　　　2008044675

This edition first published in 2009 by
**Weekly Reader® Books**
An Imprint of Gareth Stevens Publishing
1 Reader's Digest Road
Pleasantville, NY 10570-7000　USA

Copyright © 2009 by Gareth Stevens, Inc.

Executive Managing Editor: Lisa M. Herrington
Creative Director: Lisa Donovan
Senior Editor: Barbara Bakowski
Art Director: Ken Crossland
Publisher: Keith Garton
Translation: Tatiana Acosta and Guillermo Gutiérrez

Printed in the United States of America

1 2 3 4 5 6 7 8 9 10 09 08

# Table of Contents

- - - - - - - - - - - - - - -

# Contenido

**Boldface** words appear in the glossary./
Las palabras en **negrita** aparecen en el glosario.

## Small and Speedy

Meet a small dinosaur named Oviraptor (oh-vee-RAP-tor). It lived about 80 million years ago.

- - - - - - - - - - - - - -

## Pequeño y veloz

Conozcan a un pequeño dinosaurio llamado oviraptor. El oviraptor vivió hace unos 80 millones de años.

5

Oviraptor looked like a large bird.
It weighed about as much as a
nine-year-old boy.

- - - - - - - - - - - - - -

El oviraptor tenía el aspecto de un ave
de gran tamaño. Pesaba, más o menos,
lo mismo que un niño de nueve años.

Oviraptor had long legs. It could run very fast. A long tail helped the dinosaur **balance**.

- - - - - - - - - - - - - -

El oviraptor tenía unas largas patas y podía correr a gran velocidad. Su larga cola lo ayudaba a mantener el **equilibrio**.

tail/
cola

## Eat or Be Eaten!

Oviraptor was probably an **omnivore** (AHM-nee-vor). It may have eaten meat, plants, eggs, and clams.

— — — — — — — — — — — — — —

## ¡Devorar o ser devorado!

El oviraptor era, probablemente, **omnívoro**. Es posible que comiera carne, plantas, huevos y almejas.

Oviraptor had no teeth. It crushed food with its **beak** and strong jaws.

- - - - - - - - - - - - - - -

El oviraptor no tenía dientes. Trituraba la comida con su **pico** y sus poderosas mandíbulas.

beak/
pico

13

Each arm had three clawed fingers. Oviraptor fought off **predators** with its long claws.

- - - - - - - - - - - - - - -

El oviraptor tenía tres dedos con garras en cada brazo. Sus largas garras le permitían defenderse de los **depredadores**.

claws/
garras

15

## Egg Stealer or Egg Sitter?

This dinosaur's name means "egg stealer." Scientists found an Oviraptor **fossil** on top of some eggs. They thought the dinosaur was stealing the eggs to eat them.

- - - - - - - - - - - - - - -

## ¿Robar huevos o incubarlos?

El nombre de este dinosaurio significa "ladrón de huevos". Unos científicos encontraron un **fósil** de oviraptor sobre algunos huevos, y pensaron que el dinosaurio los había robado para comérselos.

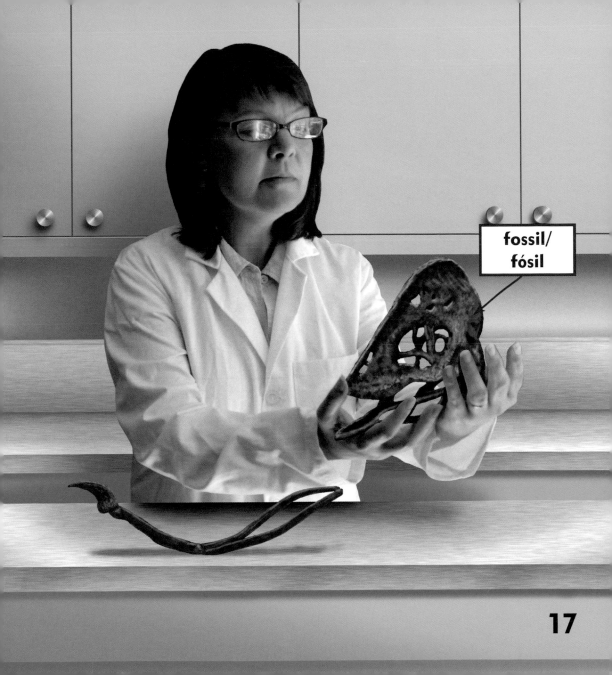

fossil/
fósil

17

Later, scientists had a new idea. Oviraptor was caring for its own eggs! It sat on a nest, just as birds do.

- - - - - - - - - - - - - -

Más adelante, los científicos cambiaron de idea. ¡El oviraptor estaba cuidando de sus propios huevos! Estaba sentado sobre ellos en el nido, como hacen las aves.

eggs/
huevos

19

Scientists have found Oviraptor fossils and eggs in Asia. Fossils help us learn about this special dinosaur.

— — — — — — — — — — — — — —

Los científicos han descubierto fósiles y huevos de oviraptor en Asia. Los fósiles nos ayudan a conocer mejor a este dinosaurio tan especial.

Russia/Rusia

Mongolia/
Mongolia

ASIA/
ASIA

China/China

North/
Norte

West/
Oeste

East/
Este

South/
Sur

KEY/CLAVE

= Oviraptor lived here/Zonas
donde vivía el oviraptor

21

# Glossary/Glosario

**balance:** to keep steady and not fall

**beak:** the hard, sharp mouthpart of an animal

**fossil:** bones or remains of animals that lived long ago

**omnivore:** an animal that eats both meat and plants

**predators:** animals that hunt and eat other animals

- - - - - - - - - - - - - - - - - - -

**depredadores:** animales que cazan y devoran a otros animales

**equilibrio:** capacidad de mantenerse en pie y no caerse

**fósiles:** huesos o restos de animales que vivieron hace mucho tiempo

**omnívoro:** animal que come carne y plantas

**pico:** parte dura y afilada de la boca de un animal

# For More Information/Más información

## Books/Libros

*Descubriendo dinosaurios con un cazador de fósiles/Discovering Dinosaurs With a Fossil Hunter.* I Like Science! Bilingual (series). Judith Williams (Enslow Publishers, 2008)

## Web Sites/Páginas web

**Dinosaurs for Kids: Oviraptor/Dinosaurios para niños: Oviraptor**
*www.kidsdinos.com/dinosaurs-for-children.php?dinosaur=Oviraptor*
This site has fun facts, illustrations, a map, and a time line./Esta página presenta datos entretenidos, ilustraciones, un mapa y una línea cronológica.

**Zoom Dinosaurs: Oviraptor/Enfoque en los dinosaurios: Oviraptor**
*www.enchantedlearning.com/subjects/dinosaurs/dinos/Oviraptor*
Find facts, pictures, maps, and printouts of Oviraptor./Encuentren datos, ilustraciones, mapas e información para imprimir sobre el oviraptor.

**Publisher's note to educators and parents:** Our editors have carefully reviewed these web sites to ensure that they are suitable for children. Many web sites change frequently, however, and we cannot guarantee that a site's future contents will continue to meet our high standards of quality and educational value. Be advised that children should be closely supervised whenever they access the Internet.

— — — — — — — — — — — — — — —

**Nota de la editorial a los padres y educadores:** Nuestros editores han revisado con cuidado las páginas web para asegurarse de que son apropiadas para niños. Sin embargo, muchas páginas web cambian con frecuencia, y no podemos garantizar que sus contenidos futuros sigan conservando nuestros elevados estándares de calidad y de interés educativo. Tengan en cuenta que los niños deben ser supervisados atentamente siempre que accedan a Internet.

# Index/Índice

## About the Author

**Joanne Mattern** has written more than 250 books for children. She has writt about weird animals, sports, world cities, dinosaurs, and many other subjects Joanne also works in her local library. She lives in New York state with her husband, four children, and assorted pets.

- - - - - - - - - - - - - - - -

## Información sobre la autora

**Joanne Mattern** ha escrito más de 250 libros para niños. Ha escrito textos sobre animales extraños, deportes, ciudades del mundo, dinosaurios y much otros temas. Además, Joanne trabaja en la biblioteca de su comunidad. Vive en el estado de Nueva York con su esposo, sus cuatro hijos y varias mascotas